WHEN YOUR TEENAGER STOPS GOING TO CHURCH

James DiGiacomo

ABBEY PRESS
St. Meinrad, Indiana 47577

Second Printing, 1982

PHOTO CREDITS: Robert Cushman Hayes, Cover; Paul Conklin, page 36; Bob Taylor, page 64.

Library of Congress Catalog Card Number
80-65401
ISBN: 0-87029-165-3

**Copyright 1980 St. Meinrad Archabbey
St. Meinrad, Indiana 47577**

CONTENTS

1. Patterns of Growth   4

2. Causes of Rejection   17

3. Messages from Parents   28

4. Religion, Faith, and Church   34

5. A Case in Point   48

6. Authority and Freedom   65

7. What to Do   78

8. Letting Go   89

CHAPTER 1
Patterns of Growth

We love to share things with our growing children. Simple things like fun, scenery, trips, laughter, good news. More serious things like ideas, ideals, values, hopes. If we are religious persons, we want to share our faith. We know that our children are more than extensions of ourselves, that they are entitled to their own lives. We hesitate to insist that they go to a certain school; we wouldn't dream of trying to force them into a particular career. Although we care very much who their friends are and what they do together, we are careful not to meddle and interfere too much in their relationships, especially as they get older. We know that in as deeply personal an area as religious faith, we are least able to impose our beliefs and practices on our sons and daughters. And yet here it is most difficult to take rejection, to accept independence, to let go. Disappointment is coupled with guilt when adolescent children stop going to church, and we ask, "Where did we go wrong? What do we do now?"

This book is an attempt to help parents deal with these questions. The issues behind the questions are universal. Protestant, Catholic, and Jewish families all experience the tensions involved in the religious socialization of children, each within the context of their particular religious tradition. The larger problems are the same for all—faith, commitment, freedom, growth, rebellion, integrity.

How much can a book like this promise? Obviously, there is no guarantee of success. Faith is free, and people are free. Nor can we offer many concrete, specific strategies for dealing with this crisis. A "how-to" book on getting people to church would be an unrealistic undertaking. What we can do is put the problem in perspective, see it in the larger context of religious commitment and isolate the real issues from the false questions that lead to dead ends. We can get help from psychology, sociology, and theology, and from a sober reflection on our own adult experience of life. From these we can draw some guidelines for action, aimed not at manipulating our children but at enabling us to offer them assistance in their own decision-making process.

If you want to understand what's happening when an adolescent undergoes a crisis of religious faith, it is necessary to know something about the challenges which face a young person on the way from childhood to maturity. Developmental psychology gives us valuable insight into this process. It doesn't tell us what to *do,* but it offers us a chance to base our prescriptions on accurate diagnoses.

A child's first religious experiences are simple and yet in their own way quite profound. Parental influences are very strong. The way Mother and Father pray and their reverent attitude in church make a lasting impact. Pictures, prayers, and gestures are very important at this stage, when religion is caught rather than taught.

As the child begins to respond to storytelling, he or she can be introduced to some of the central messages of Christianity. The child learns the Christmas story and simple biblical narratives, and participates in prayer and celebration. As children grow in understanding and begin to use language to express ideas that are less concrete and more general, they can be taught simple doctrinal formulas and the rules and customs observed by the community. This marks the beginning of religious literacy, when children find out what Christians believe and do and what is expected of them. Passing on religion in this preteen period may look deceptively easy, but these are the years when we may, without realizing it, sow the seeds of future problems. It is necessary to teach the child in very concrete terms, but this can produce in the child a very dogmatic and overly simplistic approach to religion. The nuances, the distinctions, the shadings of Christian beliefs and values — adult responses to adult questions and concerns — are missed, and sometimes all that is left is a crude literalism. In the young child, understanding is limited, and appreciation even more so.

A child's early years are years of uncritical acceptance of authority. Adults not only have all the answers; they make up the questions, too. Children are too young and too small to fight back. Most of them are not in a fighting mood, anyway; they are at the good boy/nice girl stage when the most important thing is to gain approval from parents and parent substitutes. As preteens, they will learn their lessons, say their prayers, and go to church, usually without much fuss. They are dependent on their elders not only for nurture and shelter but also for ideas and values which they accept without question, simply because they don't have the ability to sort such matters out.

In their early teen years, they begin to question, but are too young to appreciate the answers. Thirteen to sixteen year olds can ask penetrating religious questions with all the acuteness of a Dostoevsky, but lack the maturity and the experience to take in the enlightened replies. They are not yet ready to take responsibility for their own beliefs, their world view, their system of values. Such a level of autonomy is rarely attained before late adolescence or young adulthood. But they are in a transitional phase, and a painful one it sometimes is, not so much for them but for the sensitive and responsible adults who care for them. Some parents respond by establishing an authoritarian milieu where dissent is stifled and conformity rewarded. This may help them more easily weather this phase, though a high price will be exacted, the stifling of a child's individuality in coming to a personal faith commitment.

The way a child is introduced to religion both reflects and affects the type of religion the child will embrace. The Roman Catholic Church presents an interesting case study in the matter. For decades American Catholics knew a church that was monolithic, authoritarian, simplistic, unsophisticated. It had many positive characteristics, too: loyalty, commitment, a sensitivity to the transcendent and the sacred. As long as this kind of faith predominated, it was fairly easy for Catholics to socialize their young, *for this was the kind of religion that children could understand.* When many adult Catholics, with the encouragement of the Second Vatican Council, began to move toward a more mature style and level of faith, they naturally attempted to bring their children along with them. In many cases, they succeeded, but often they failed, and for a variety of reasons. Sometimes the way religion is taught and celebrated in the parish fails to reflect the way it is perceived at home. Either the parents are out in front of the parish priests and the school, or they are clinging to the old ways while the church and school try to implement the spirit of renewal. By the time the children reach high school age, a third kind of tension may develop. The youngster may find at school a kind of celebration and a level of theological awareness at odds with that encountered at home and/or in the parish church. Such differences are unsettling to adolescents, many of whom resent the fact that all the adults in their lives do not tell them the same things. They could more gracefully accept this if they were capable of discriminating judgement, but they are not. Besides, all those people — parents, priests, teachers — represent *authority:* and if the authorities can't get together and make up their minds, why should they listen to any of them? This experience of receiving conflicting signals from authority figures either brings on youthful alienation from church or plays into the hands of those youngsters who are looking for an excuse to reject religion.

It is vitally important that parents check to see that the religion they present at home is being reinforced in church and in religious education classes, and *vice versa.* They need to find out how effectively they and their children's teachers are communicating with the kids and with each other. Sometimes the youth are way ahead of their parents and teachers; they ask serious, even precocious questions and are scandalized at the poverty of thought reflected in the answers given them. Sometimes it's just the other way around: the teachers are far over the kids' heads, talking at a level of sophistication far beyond their students' capacity to understand or appreciate. Ideally, parents and teachers should be able to discuss these problems, but often they are unable to do so. One may perceive the other as a threat, and the dialogue either fails to get off the ground or degenerates into active or passive hostility rooted in misunderstanding. Often the occasion simply doesn't arise: the parent never visits the school or inquires into the religion program. The son or daughter doesn't talk about religion at home, because he or she has stopped talking about everything except on a superficial level.

As a Catholic religion teacher of teenagers for many years, I am astounded at how few parents show an active concern about the substance and style of what my colleagues and I are teaching their children at such an impressionable and critical age. Recently, the father of one of my students came to the conclusion that I was not faithful to Catholic doctrine in my teaching. We disagreed on theology but readily came to an agreement that his son should be kept out of my classes. He said, "I hope you're not offended." I replied, "Of course not. This is not a dispute between personalities, but a matter of principle. I wish that you and I, who are both serious Catholics, could agree in our perception of our faith; and I would enjoy teaching your son. But as long as we cannot, it is your duty as a parent to take this step. I wish more parents were as actively concerned as you are."

Sometimes it is impossible to get parents, ministers, and teachers to say the same things in the same way to growing children. Pluralism is a phenomenon that is here to stay. It is our task to help the young deal responsibly with this pluralism. They must learn to accept the fact that adult Christians, even members of the same denomination or worshipers at the same church, differ among themselves in the way they interpret and practice their common faith. It is more difficult, but not impossible, to bring up children this way. In preparing them for citizenship, for example, we don't program them to be intolerant, dogmatic bigots. We teach them to respect those of other political persuasions, and to accept those who differ with them. Such distinctions do not come easily for the adolescent mind, which is more comfortable with good guy and bad guy categories. But they are not going to be adolescents forever, and it's never too early to teach a tolerance that doesn't have to be a mushy relativism.

There is no denying that teaching and sharing religion this way involves risk. Tell youngsters that not everything in Scripture happened just the way it is written and they hear you saying, "The Bible isn't true; it's just a bunch of stories." Admit that not attending church isn't automatically a sin, and they conclude, "We don't have to go to church." Share your reservations about an official position of the church, and they agree, "Our church leaders have no right to tell people what to do." Tell them that others besides Christians can be saved, and now they understand, "You don't have to belong to any church; all you gotta do is be a good person." These are examples of what we mean when we say that religion, when passed on from adults to young people, loses a lot in the translation.

But what's the alternative? The kind of religion they understand—simplistic, legalistic, tribalistic (the kind that Freud and Marx knew and criticized) is the kind that they will feel compelled to reject, sooner rather than later. What they need is not to understand, but to be in touch with adults who work at understanding and who, besides being believers, come across as intellectually honest, open, and forthright. For youth lean on their elders, and will until they pass to a more mature level of faith at which they take responsibility for themselves and their commitments. At that point, they will have been well served if you and the other adult believers in their lives have been models not of unthinking conformity but of personal conviction and free choice.

Remember these key words: growth, evolution, development; and observe that all these ideas are dynamic not static. Your children are growing, the church is evolving, and if your own development has ceased, you're, in effect, dead. Christianity is not a mere collection of doctrines and rules that are fixed forever in unchanging formulas. Children pass through phases of development that are mental and emotional as well as physical. You, as a mature person, are also changing, though at a much more deliberate pace. Does the Christian faith mean the same thing to you now as it did when you were 27? When you were 17? When you were 7? The faith hasn't changed, but you have. And at every new stage of life—adolescence, young adulthood, maturity—you have to develop a new set of questions, new responses, new appreciation. If Christianity is not just a collection of words but a way of relating to all of life, then something is wrong when eleven year olds start complaining, "We've heard it all before." Of course they have, but that's not the point. They've heard the *words*—salvation, sin, freedom, life, love, forgiveness, community, friendship—but these have to be experienced and grasped anew, over and over again, as they progress to new levels of maturity.

Adolescents are engaged in a process of reexamining and restructuring so much in their lives. Their values, their ideals, their beliefs, their prejudices, and most of all their relationships, are coming under more and more critical scrutiny. This process will determine, to a great extent, whether they will be idealistic or cynical, generous or selfish, self-esteeming or self-hating, refined or vulgar, hopeful or despairing. Teenagers confront a whole new range of concerns: What do I want out of life? What kind of person do I want to be? Shall I join the believers or the skeptics? The do-gooders or the go-getters? Shall I accept the world as it is and adjust to it, or try to change it even a little bit? Is there more to living than adjusting and surviving? What is love, and how can you tell? How can I accept myself when there's so much wrong with me?

Religion should help teenagers deal with these concerns. Nine year olds cannot be taught the answers to such questions, because they're too young even to ask them. But teenagers can at least be helped to put the questions into words and confront the answers given by Christ and his followers. Whether they accept them or not is up to them; they are free. They ought to experience religion at this age as at least one answer to the large question mark that is themselves. They might reject it, but at least they could take it seriously. And they could never again honestly dismiss it as mere kid stuff.

The people, young and old, who stay with religion and stay with church are those who perceive these as an *enrichment*. If I see myself as being a better or richer person for having been part of church, then I am not going to reject it for trivial reasons. Those who walk away from the Church are almost universally those who during their religious formation never made the vital connections with themselves, with others, or with God that are the very stuff of religion. When we take something seriously, we don't abandon it except for serious reasons.

Once in a while you meet a refreshingly honest person, like the advertising executive who confided to me that he left the Catholic Church when they put the Mass into English: "When I found out what they were saying, I realized I didn't believe it." Actually, his case was a good deal more complex than that; but at least he did a very unusual thing. He diagnosed the problem as being within himself. Teenagers and young adults who drop out of church almost always place the reason elsewhere and seldom admit that the problem is usually somewhere within themselves.

Why are people, especially young people, so scandalized at finding that the Church is filled with sinful people who don't measure up to their Christian ideals? Certainly Jesus didn't promise such a Church; he made it very clear that there would be plenty of chaff among the wheat. These same young people, in their history courses, learn that after 200 years the American people are still trying unsuccessfully to achieve their constitutional ideals of universal freedom, equality, and justice. In the face of such bad news, do they emigrate? No, they stay, hoping that things will get better and maybe deciding to try to help.

What they fail to grasp about the Church is that it too is growing and evolving; it is not a finished reality, perfect and fully realized. It is a pilgrim people, occasionally losing their way, stumbling into dead ends, but always on the march to something better. Since it is made up of people, it is always engaged in a process of growth, of self-criticism, of reassessment and change. Were it otherwise, it would not be a living thing; it would be a museum, not the Body of Christ.

Religious faith and church membership is not something we can give our children once and for all when they are very young and admonish them not to lose, the way we warn them not to lose their gloves. Gloves get lost, and so does faith, but not in the same way. Gloves just have to be held onto, but faith has to grow just as we grow, or it dies. A child's faith is insufficient for an adolescent, and adolescent faith cannot survive adulthood. Adult religion cannot be outgrown, but childish religiosity can and should be left behind.

CHAPTER 2
Causes of Rejection

When a teenager stops going to church, it can mean any one or a number of many things.

The least serious motive could be dissatisfaction not with religion or Church in general, but just with the local situation. There are youngsters who, like many adults, have a genuine hunger for religious experience and nourishment but cannot find it in their local church community. Their problem is not with Christianity but with a particular group of Christians. If you listen to kids who are drifting away, they'll say that this is their situation. They lack patience with leaders whom they contend do not lead, or with an adult community that they feel does not know how to reach out to them. Don't accept this explanation too easily; the chances are that the real problem lies elsewhere.

Sometimes the problem may be simple,

old-fashioned laziness. Just as they find it hard to study, to clean their rooms, to do the chores, or to get out of bed, so teenagers lack the energy to go to church. Of course, it's not physical energy but psychic energy that's lacking. Usually it's a question of motivation. The same boy who rejects study or worship because it's "boring" will put up with endless, grinding repetition and mind-numbing routine in order to make an athletic squad. And the girl who seems unable to concentrate or cope with monotony will practice endlessly, showing incredible endurance in order to win a majorette competition.

The rejection of adult religious values may be part of the pattern that leads to rebellion in other areas. In adolescence and young adulthood, the testing of limits is part of the thrust toward independence and autonomy. It is not unusual, nor should we be surprised when youth overstep the bounds. When your son or daughter stops going to church, see if it is an isolated problem, or if it is part of a pattern of rebelliousness. Your child may be trying to find him- or herself by rejecting you. In this case, religion and church are not on trial; they are simply caught in the crossfire between the generations.

This rebellion may be an individual matter, but it is much more likely to be a group phenomenon. Throughout adolescence, but especially in the early teens, peer pressure is tremendous—often it is *the* problem. Youngsters at this

CAUSES OF REJECTION

age often lack the solid core of identity and sense of self needed to stand up to social pressures. Just a few years ago it was *your* influence and pressure that got them to do many things, including going to church. You still have a lot of clout, but now you have formidable rivals, not only the peer group in school and neighborhood, but the television, popular music, and movie industries that so often promote values and practices not in conformity with Christianity. Developmental psychologists point out that adolescents are normally incapable of principled thinking or behavior. Kids want desperately to be accepted, and the price is conformity. If your child's friends don't go to church—if "putting down" religion is one of their group hobbies—then it's hard for your son or daughter to stand up to that. He or she will offer all kinds of rationalizations for dropping out of church—adult religious hypocrisy, poor preaching, insensitive clergy—but the real reason is the simple inability to withstand group pressure.

A deeper, more troublesome cause of leaving church may be the feeling that, for them, participation in formal religion is hypocritical. They may feel guilty and uncomfortable in attending church if their lives are not being lived in conformity with the gospels. Youths face strong temptations toward excessive drinking, drug abuse, sexual experimentation, petty thievery, vandalism; and the pressure of their peers to engage in such activities can be overwhelming. If a youth succumbs to such temptations, he or she may feel hypocritical in attending church. Unfortunately, many people both young and old think of church attendance as a statement of how they live, rather than of how they want to live. They don't take seriously Jesus' concern for cheating tax collectors, prostitutes, and doubters, and the amount of time he spent with them.

Kids with serious problems in the above areas need help. Jesus specialized in helping sinners, and when he went looking for them he didn't go to the temple or synagogue. The Church has many dedicated people working in youth ministry who try to reach out to such young people. For them, questions of formal religious practices and beliefs become relevant only after much more basic problems have been confronted and dealt with.

A less disturbing but no less deep-seated problem that may lead young people to drop out of church is the absence of any consciously religious dimension in their everyday lives. Perhaps they seldom or never pray. God is remote and unreal, a name for a rumor spread by other people, not someone they experience or with whom they converse. Their ambitions and desires may be totally materialistic; they never confront the larger questions of life, the issues of meaning and significance. There is no quiet space in their existence where they can confront themselves in a thoughtful, serious way. They

CAUSES OF REJECTION

find their fun and their friends, and pursue their interests and activities outside church and church groups. For such youths, what can churchgoing be but an empty, formalistic exercise answering not to their own needs but to other people's expectations? So they drop out. There is a kind of consistency in their doing so. They have grasped part of a truth that often evades conventionally religious people: formal religious practice is meaningless when there is no resonance in the rest of one's life. If people live without God, what meaning is there in their participation in organized religious activities? Of course, when teenagers drop out for this reason, they don't explain it the way we just did. Rather, they rationalize the religious vacuum within themselves with defensive statements like "Why do I have to go to church with all these hypocrites who talk about love and then cut off one another's cars in the parking lot after services? I'd rather just be a good person."

When such statements are made, many adults—including myself, on more than one occasion—try to defend churchgoers and what goes on in church. This misses the mark entirely. The issue here is not church and the people in it, but the young dropout whose rejection of and attacks on religion provide a smoke screen for the emptiness and superficiality of his or her own life.

One of the reasons young people stop attending church lies neither in the church nor in the young person but in a larger sociological phenomenon. This is the widening gap between the values of the dominant culture and the values of Christianity. There has always been a division, but lately it seems to have become more pronounced. The values of our consumer society are getting, owning, enjoying, producing, competing, winning. These put a high premium on aggressiveness, self-satisfaction, status, security. When a Christian church gets beyond pious platitudes and bourgeois piety to preaching the gospel of Jesus Christ, it looks and sounds countercultural. The Church tells anyone who is really listening that the worth of a person cannot be measured by money or the things he or she owns; that frugality is to be preferred to conspicuous consumption; that we are our brothers' and sisters' keepers; that justice and honesty are not to be compromised in the struggle for status and security.

This cultural gap is perhaps most obvious in the matter of sex. As youngsters grow up they learn that the Church has strict standards of sexual morality. Even allowing for differences among Christians—and some are quite significant—it is safe to say that, as a group, they stand for a set of sexual values that is increasingly under attack in the wider community. The Church's stand on premarital sex and fidelity in marriage, for example, is consistently and blatantly contradicted in most movie and television entertainment and in the lyrics of music popular with teenagers. The trivialization of sex, the attack on marriage, the rejection of anything that smacks of self-control or postponement of gratification, all conspire to get across the message that traditional standards of sexual responsibility are at best passé and, at worst, puritanical. Add to this the enormous peer pressure on teenagers and you have a situation where young people are increasingly pulled in two opposite directions. What they hear at home and in church school is worlds removed from what they hear in the "outside" world.

Does this affect churchgoing among the young? How could it be otherwise? If the world of rock and disco and TV makes sense to you, then what goes on in church must seem nonsensical. The clash is, for the most part, unconscious, but no less real. Adults are used to moving in and out of conflicting worlds and roles and keeping their balance in the process, but it is much more difficult for adolescents to do this. They are confused by the conflicting signals that come their way from different segments of society. Their response is at best ambivalent.

People in their forties and fifties grew up in a world where much of the surrounding popular culture was either neutral or gave support to what their parents and teachers were telling them. It's not that way, anymore. Today's Christian parents need to provide motivation and encouragement for religious practice and commitment, and they must do so against formidable opposition from the surrounding culture. Religion challenges people to make choices, to take stands, to affirm values. Parents must know who they are, what they want, and what they stand for in order to help their children do the same, against heavy odds.

In discussing reasons why young people drop out of church, we must address ourselves to a fact that shows up in curiously different ways. Religion is, fundamentally, an *adult* phenomenon. Left to themselves, children and adolescents would never start churches. When mothers brought children to Jesus, the apostles told them not to bother their master. Jesus didn't teach children, and he didn't organize a teen club. The New Testament is devoid of preaching or writing directed explicitly to the young; it's all grown-up stuff.

Religion addresses itself to the most fundamental questions and the deepest longings of the human heart. Questions like: Does life have any purpose? Is anyone in charge, or are we the products of chance? Is death stronger than life? Is existence ultimately comedy or tragedy? These are adult questions. Teenagers ask them occasionally, but for the most part such concerns do not absorb their attention.

This is not to say that religion is not for the young. But it has to be adapted, and it's bound to lose something in the process. Growing children have always been bored and distracted during worship. There are some people in ministry who are skilled in conducting liturgies for the young, and help has come their way lately in the form of celebrations composed with youngsters' needs in mind. But conducting church services for the young is like teaching history and civics to grammar school children. They can learn names and dates and can absorb a simplified version of issues and events, but that's all. And of course, left to themselves, they'd prefer ball scores and situation comedies to analyzing the causes of the Civil War. But we know they're not always going to be kids, that in a few years they'll be able to vote, so we tell them that social studies is important, and we try to teach them. We don't *ask* them if they want to do social studies; we just *do* them. And if they're bored, we try to make the subject more interesting, but we don't give up. The process of socialization, for citizenship as well as for church membership, inevitably includes involvement with concerns that are specifically adult and not of immediate interest to the young. That makes for resistance and lack of motivation, which we can sometimes minimize but never eliminate entirely.

There is one last cause of rejection, and it is a curious variation of the religion-for-adults problem. At first sight it seems just the opposite. We are referring to the impression, widespread among adolescents, that religion is for children: church is something you outgrow. For some teenagers, one of the great things about emerging from childhood is that it gives you a chance to emerge from religious concerns as well. An excerpt from a letter by a college junior will illustrate this. The collegian had been a student of this writer at a Catholic high school, and he was talking about the fact that many of his peers had dropped out of church:

> Why does it happen this way? Of the believers in (high school) freshman year, very few remain in senior year. I have seen this in good friends of mine time after time. It is a process. They call it "growing up," "finding out what it's all about," "facing reality," "maturing." I had a good friend in freshman year—a wonderful guy whom I'd known a long time in my neighborhood. He was a believer, a very good Catholic, active in the parish and in the Prep Sodality. He changed. By senior year he'd lost his religion, adopted a new outlook on life, found a new set of values, a new set of friends (not including me). I met him not long ago. I said at one point that he had changed a great deal since the frosh days at Prep. He replied, "Yes, I have changed. I've grown up. When are you going to change?"

What is it about religion that makes it seem like kid stuff, even to religious people? When religious education coordinators want to attract a large crowd of adults on a weekday evening what topic do they announce? Something about young people and religion, not about adults. For reasons too numerous to name, religion in the United States is a child-centered phenomenon. No matter how many official church documents pronounce adult religious education as the church's top priority, the majority of men and women in or out of the pews will think of religion as something you learn when you're a kid, and of church as being a place to go "for the sake of the children." That's why many young couples who have drifted away from the Church persist in bringing their children to be baptized — not just to placate the grandparents, but from a deep-seated notion that religion is something you should give your children even though you've dropped it in your own life.

Let us move now from a consideration of young people and their attitudes to the question of adult beliefs and religious convictions. We have said that parents cannot give children what they as adults do not have, and so it is important for parents to take a careful look at their own reasons for going to church.

CHAPTER 3
Messages from Parents

Parents constantly send messages to their children. Children learn how to live as much from their parents' example as from what their parents say. Every survey taken confirms that parental influence far outweighs every other factor in the religious development of the young. The style and quality of parental religious attitudes and practices—of the mother *and* of the father—are good indicators of whether and how the child will be religious. This is *not* to say that parents are always at fault when things go wrong. There are many other influences on young people, and many of them militate against growth in religious faith. Even when parents do everything right, their efforts can be frustrated by forces outside the home and by the free will of their children. But the messages sent by parents are critical in the child's religious development.

A few years ago a Roman Catholic priest told me of the following encounter with a woman parishioner:

WOMAN: Father, you must help me. My 16-year-old son refuses to go to Mass. He says he doesn't get anything out of it.
PRIEST: Do *you* go?
WOMAN: No.
PRIEST: Why not?
WOMAN: I don't get anything out of it.
PRIEST: Well, if you don't go, I don't see how you can expect your son to go. Why should he?
WOMAN: His father goes like clockwork!

What messages are these parents sending their son?

Parents concerned that their son or daughter is not attending church can begin by asking themselves why they go to church. Do both parents attend regularly? Do you go out of habit? Fear? Hope? Do you go because it is expected, or to give example to your children, or to keep peace in the family? Do you feel a personal need to worship, to feed an important part of yourself?

Teenagers want to know how their parents' lives are different for having gone to church? What impact does religion have on the way they live? They may not always ask these questions in an honest spirit, to be sure; often they are looking for rationalizations of their own laziness and for excuses to give in to their low BTP (Boredom Tolerance Point). But they are good questions. Centuries before Christ, the prophets of Israel protested against empty temple worship devoid of honesty, compassion, and social justice. Jesus, in this same spirit, warns us that not everyone who calls him lord will enter the kingdom of heaven, but only those who do his father's will.

Adult religious hypocrisy is a word teenagers throw around all too freely; it is a reason regularly given for not attending church. To the immature mind, all the people in church must be either spotless saints or hardened hypocrites; there are no in-betweens. Such thinking is characteristic of adolescence. If the Apostles had been teenagers, they would have banned all sinners from the church. Such self-serving intolerance carries the message: "I have very high standards for churches; if they aren't perfect, I can't stand them. When they get their act together, maybe I'll think about coming back. I'm all right, but they'll have to shape up."

Allowing for the immaturity of teenagers, we can still take their questions seriously. What effect does church have on *your* life? Does it give you a little more hope or deep down joy and peace than you would have otherwise? Does it give you resources for living in these difficult times? Are your moral standards any different from those of the nonchurchgoers? Are you conscious of striving, in virtue of your faith, for ideals of honesty and integrity beyond the ordinary and the mediocre? Does your church experience lead you to be actively concerned with the welfare of the needy, the lonely, the rejected? Does Christianity help you to overcome the impulses to racism and prejudice that are in the air we breathe? In a word, are your values and lifestyle perceptibly influenced by the faith that you profess? Is your weekly attendance at church an isolated event unrelated to the rest of your life, or is it part of a religious commitment that plays a significant role in your concerns, life-style, and participation in the life of your community? Your children already know the answer to these questions, and it is probably influencing, for good or ill, their receptivity to religious education and formation.

"But I'm so busy!" To be sure, some people have less time and energy at their disposal than others. A man or woman holding two jobs to keep up with inflation can hardly be faulted for not answering the pastor's call for volunteers to work with the youth group. Such things are relative. What is constant is the fact that people make time for the things they think important: they set priorities. In the battle for your time, does religion always lose?

We are trying to get beyond the notion of church as spiritual filling station, where we fill up the tank once a week and then forget about it. Youngsters feel that many adults do it this way, and they look upon such churchgoing as sterile. They don't spell it out this clearly in their minds, and they can't articulate it, but it probably underlies much of their apathy and resistance. This is one case where thinking small may be counterproductive. If our religious expectations of ourselves and our children are too small, they may appear inconsequential, or—in teen language—"no big deal."

Parents would do well to take a look at the church they're asking their sons and daughters to attend, to assess just what it is that they are anxious to have their children involved in.

At the local level, do those engaged in ministry give genuine religious leadership, or are they primarily managers or business administrators? Are the people responsive to Christian ideals? Can it be said of them, "See how they love one another?" Or are they an assembly of individuals closed in on themselves? Is Sunday worship at least sometimes the occasion of genuine religious experience, or is it a joyless, calculated routine? Are the parishioners better people for going to this church? Does the religious community have an impact for good on the wider community?

If your local church scores high on quality of religious experience and concern, you have a lot going for you when you seek to involve your son or daughter. You're giving them a chance to plug into something that's alive. If your church scores low, you have a problem. Serious religious people bring their own strength or fervor to a feeble, sputtering enterprise. They can draw nourishment from an uninspired liturgical performance, stay alive even among people who are just going through the motions, preserve interest despite the surrounding apathy. They can even improve the situation. But this is a lot to ask of youth; those who are uninterested or alienated or suspicious will more likely be turned off all the more.

In trying to keep our children interested and involved in religion, we should not underestimate the obstacles, which won't go away just because we ignore them. We may have to go looking for a more supportive environment, searching for a local church that communicates itself as a joyous gathering of those who take seriously the following of Christ in all aspects of their lives. When young people get the message that church really makes a difference, they'll almost always readily involve themselves.

CHAPTER 4
Religion, Faith, and Church

When you picked up this book, you were probably looking for some down-to-earth, practical advice on how to keep your son or daughter from becoming a negative church statistic. We're trying not to be too theoretical, and we hope to get practical and specific before we finish. But hopefully it is clear that you can't just settle for asking how to get your kid to church; you have to sort out for yourself just what this whole church thing is about. It means so many different things to so many people! Religion, faith, church, three realities different yet the same, each requiring an individual to come to grips with it.

Religion
Most people, when they hear this word, think of activities—saying prayers, attending

RELIGION, FAITH, AND CHURCH

services, joining a religious group. That's part of it, but we have seen that this can be very superficial or conventional activity, with little depth or personal engagement, done out of habit or to meet other people's expectations. At a deeper level, being religious means being involved in matters of larger meaning, of ultimate concern. When a person becomes concerned not only with practical, day-to-day matters like paying bills, staying healthy, holding a job, keeping house, and deciding where to go on vacation, but also with the purpose and meaning of existence, the place of God in one's life, and his or her eternal destiny, then that person is being religious. Even before he or she picks an answer, it's the *questions* that matter. Or, from another angle, it's a matter of what you *want* out of life. If all one wants is what the stores and banks and insurance companies promise (which is considerable), then such a person may not be ready for religion.

The difference is graphically presented in an incident in St. Luke's Gospel. Two men interrupt Jesus and ask him to arbitrate a property dispute between them. In reply, he tells the story of a farmer who had the kind of problem every farmer would love to have — a harvest so big that his barns were too small. So he tears down his barns, builds bigger ones, and stores the produce. Then he complacently announces that he will eat, drink, and relax, because he's got it made. And God calls him a fool, because

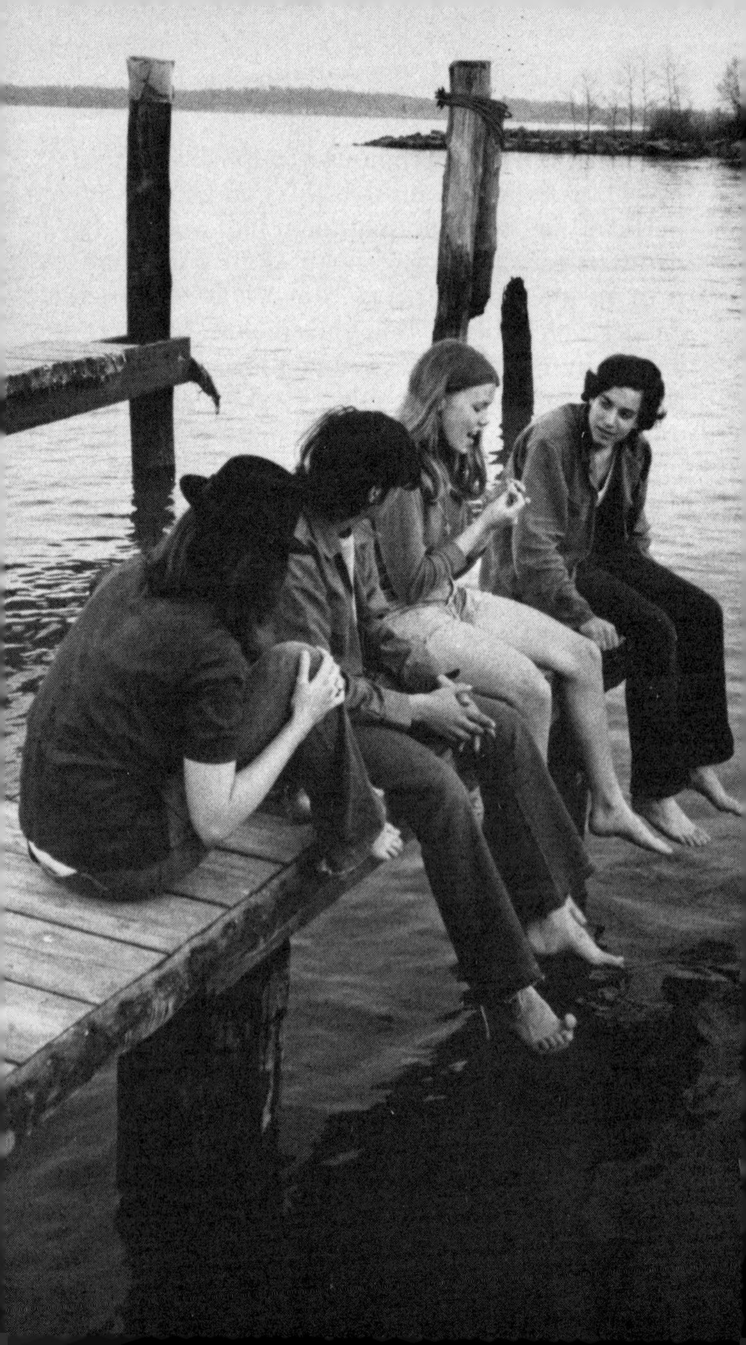

he's going to die that very night, and he can't take his riches with him. This is Jesus' way of telling us that there are matters more important than the size of our bank accounts.

Jesus doesn't criticize people for worrying about where the next meal is coming from or how they're going to pay the bills, but he invites them to go beyond these preoccupations to weightier matters. The day after he fed the crowd with free bread, he points out to them that they are already hungry again; how would they like to have some bread which would let them be hungry no more? Their fathers ate manna in the desert and are dead. He offers the bread of life; whoever eats it shall live forever.

Jesus cures a blind man, and calls himself the light of the world; follow him, and you will not walk in darkness. Before he cures a paralyzed man, he forgives him his sins and reminds us that there are worse things than being deprived of the use of arms and legs. You could be shriveled up inside, your heart contracted by selfishness and greed, unable to love or to care.

The overemphasis on externals that characterizes American life makes it difficult for many to deal with the deeper levels of existence. There are an unlimited number of bright, shiny, noisy trifles available in a consumer society to distract a person from ever getting below the surface of existence. You could starve to death without ever knowing you were hungry. Many young people seem to sense this; how else explain their yearning for solitude and a chance for contemplation? Consumerism reduces life to getting and owning and using and enjoying; religion reminds us that we are meant for more than this. As Augustine puts it, our hearts are restless until they rest in God. There is a transcendent dimension to life that humans ignore at their own risk. "What does it profit a man if he gains the whole world and loses himself?" Religion is concerned with the transcendent.

Religious people want *more.* More what? Security? Yes, but that could be misleading. There is a temptation to reduce the religious quest to a kind of celestial insurance policy: "Pie in the sky, by and by, when you die." That's what kids put down when they call religion a crutch. Religion as a search for security is a static concept that closes off possibilities, that breeds complacency and mediocrity. You can see this in people and in churches that are closed in on themselves, lacking in social concern or compassion, literally "out of this world." This is what religion can slip into and settle for, if it does not go a step further, to *faith.*

Faith

Faith rescues religion from narcissistic, self-seeking mediocrity. It bids us be open to adventure, to the unforeseen, to possibilities undreamt of. The Bible gives us Abraham as a man of faith. God invites him to leave the familiarity, the predictability, and the comfort of

Haran, where he had worked for years to bring himself and his family to a position of prominence and prosperity, and to set out on a difficult and dangerous journey to parts unknown. If Abraham had been without faith, he would have held on to his security; he would have never left Haran and become the father of a great people.

Jesus calls a group of young men who could have led normal lives of conventional respectability, and offers them a vagabond existence fraught with danger and beset by opposition, ending in violent persecution and death. This is security? Jean Danielou sums it up very well:

> Is it more comfortable to be a Christian than to be not Christian? As for me, I am not persuaded of that at all. What I am convinced of, in contrast, is that the condition of a Christian, to the extent that being a Christian means agreeing to be at the disposition of someone else, is something extraordinarily uncomfortable! And you know it very well . . . Once you set the wheels you don't know how far you're liable to go. . . . We know, as Riviere put it so well, that "love involves staggering complications." We are always taking something upon ourselves when we introduce somebody else into our life, even from the human point of view. We know that no longer shall we be altogether our own man. Therein lies the adventuresomeness of human love as well as the self-sacrifice involved in it . . . Well, then! To allow Christ to enter our life is a terrible, terrible, terrible risk. What will it lead to? And faith—is precisely that.

This understanding of faith is not the conventional one. Faith is closely connected with religious identity; I am a Christian if I believe in Christ. But religion, in this country, is largely a middle-class phenomenon, a conventional part of American life. There's nothing wrong with being conventional, but the fact is that in Christianity, as in its spiritual parent, Judaism, there has always been a tension between faith and the established order.

The Israelites are at their best in the desert, a breakaway people recently escaped from bondage, on the move toward a distant goal. The prophets repeatedly challenge the religious formalism practiced by those who have "settled down." Christianity is founded by a decidedly unconventional Jew, catches on with the poor and the oppressed, flourishes under persecution, and goes stale when Constantine makes it part of the establishment. Fortunately, the prophetic element never completely disappears in the life of the Church, but it can be almost invisible at certain times and in certain places.

Do you perceive your religious faith as making you more adventuresome, or more stodgy? Does it challenge as well as comfort you? Does it offer risk and sacrifice as well as security?

When you dated your spouse and took the big step of getting married and then accepted children, wasn't it exciting? It was hard and demanding and sometimes it was frightening, but it wasn't boring. Faith is somewhat like that. It's a leap into the unknown, at the bidding of Another.

It is normal for adolescents to be adventuresome, to take risks. If they were as careful and prudent as their elders, there would be fewer accidents, but there would be less excitement and probably less progress, too. One reason many young people are repelled by faith and religion is because the believers always seem more cautious and calculating than the skeptics. That's why, in religion classrooms, the most outspoken youngsters are usually those who have rejected official religious beliefs and practices.

Living up to Christ's values and ideals in today's world calls for courage and individuality. Being honest, not using people, being sexually responsible, caring for others, resisting peer pressure—these take strong faith and a firm backbone. To be a Christian in a phony, plastic world is to be truly countercultural, to swim against the tide.

Faith is more than a belief in doctrines, though it includes that. It is a belief not in something but in Someone; it builds on trust and it issues in commitment. If that sounds like falling in love and getting married, it's no coincidence. But for any of this to happen, there must be an encounter, a meeting of persons. That is why we placed so much stress, earlier, on the need for religious experience, especially the experience of prayer. The young person who drifts away from church is described as "losing" his or her faith, but that may be inaccurate. There may have been religious instruction and religious activity, but no faith. There may have been recitation of pious formulas, but no real prayer. God may be just a rumor, someone that other people are always talking about but who has never been encountered in a personal way. There comes a point in a person's life — and it seems to come earlier and earlier — when, without faith, church becomes meaningless. And that shouldn't surprise us, when we consider what church is all about.

Church

Just as faith is about a *who* before it's about a *what,* so also church is a *who* before it's a *where.* It's a group of "faith-full" people who share a belief, a trust, and a commitment. They live a life of faith, and they live it *together.* Religion, for them, is not a purely individualistic thing; it's a group experience. These statements are very basic theological affirmations which most adults have no trouble accepting, but which adolescents often find very difficult. They sound much too idealistic, too far removed from reality. Do the people who attend church on Sunday really share a living faith? Aren't many of them there out of pure habit, and don't they show it when they are inert and unresponsive to leadership and to one another? Can we honestly call the

Sunday congregation a *community?* Wouldn't we be better off staying away from that crowd of hypocrites and praying to God all by ourselves in a quiet place?

These objections should be taken seriously, but critically, too. Of course our description of church is idealistic. Rare is the group that measures up to the ideal, or even comes close. On the other hand, most churches are not nearly as bad as teenagers think. Growing young people are at a stage of life when inconsistencies, especially by adults and adult institutions, are especially intolerable. They see the warts and very little else. Youthful idealism is a beautiful thing, but it can be unforgiving and rigid and blind to genuine virtue. Adults who haven't necessarily settled for mediocrity but who have developed compassion for human weakness know that in this group of worshipers, so plodding and uninspired on the surface, there are cases of unselfish and quiet heroism which, without faith, might be just quiet desperation. Didn't Jesus say he was looking for sinners? Going to church isn't the same as saying, "I'm okay": it means, "I'm looking for healing, for strength, for nourishment." The people who show up on Sunday need all of that and more. They need one another.

Our faith tells us that these people, with all their good and bad points, have not come together just on their own. They have been called. It is God who creates church, and God who gives it life and enables it to grow. He doesn't force anything on us; we are free to respond or not. But when we answer his call and join in church, we become part of something bigger than ourselves. There is available to us a life and a strength and a power that we could never attain by ourselves.

Students of theology will recognize the above as simply a restatement of the doctrine, accepted by all Christian bodies, of the primacy of grace. It is an old doctrine, as old as St. Paul's statement that no one can say "Jesus is Lord" except by the Holy Spirit. But it is not a familiar belief to most adolescents, even those who have received years of religious instruction. Most teenagers, even those who have very little individuality, are very individualistic when it comes to religion. They think it's *their* job to choose a religion or a church, to find God, to become good persons. This is put very well in a fascinating film which depicts a conversation between God the father and God the son about the trouble that humans were giving them:

SON: They're so bent on perfecting themselves . . . they're closing everything off.

FATHER: If they would just relax, we could do it all for them.

To come to church is to admit that I can't do it all by myself, that I need God and other people. It means letting others into my life and being at their disposition; and that's uncomfortable. An adolescent is a person who was recently a child and is trying to become an adult, who thinks that being free means not listening to anybody and being on his or her own. That's why adolescents are not the easiest people to live with. Part of growing up is rearranging relationships with others, and it doesn't come easily.

A church is supposed to be a community. Adults find it hard to achieve community, especially in today's society; their efforts often fall short. Achieving community in church is made even more difficult by the fact that not everyone who comes there is looking for it. Some people just want a quiet place to say their prayers. They don't mind a little sermon, as long as it's not about the real needs of real people in the real world and our obligation to try to do something for them. For these folks, who are quite religious in their own way, consolation and security are in, but challenge and change are out. They have a very private God who concerns himself only with a very circumscribed area of life called the sacred. It may come as a surprise to more social-minded Christians that when the Catholic Church restored to its liturgy the ancient custom of the greeting of peace, problems were experienced and that they have not all gone away. "Why must I interrupt my prayers and talk to people?" "What about germs?" "And who are these people, anyway? I don't even know their names."

Such questions are not out of place. There is an opinion which holds that liturgy cannot create community; that, on the contrary, only community can create liturgy. When people have nothing in common except the fact that they turn up for church every week, a ritualized greeting can seem artificial and forced.

The Church is trying to say something very important but easily lost sight of: religion, in the Christian sense, means relating not only to God but to other people. Church is community, or perhaps better said, church is *becoming* community. Youth in its adolescent immaturity can find this very hard to accept. To cope with its limitations in a constructive way, teenagers need to see church not as a monument, a finished or perfect thing, but rather a living body, experiencing the pains of growth. We make allowances for adolescents when they do crazy things, because we know that they're still young, not mature adults. Can they do the same for church? Just as people are never finished products (unless they're dead), so the Church will always be unfinished, with cracks and flaws and gaps waiting to be filled. The Church is a pilgrim people on a journey; it should be no surprise that we haven't yet arrived. As we stumble along, the Church has a job so important that it's worth doing badly. It is to put us in touch with God. If it succeeds in that, then we can put up with all the other failures.

What kind of God is the Church supposed

to put us in touch with? All the people who show up on Sunday for the right reasons are looking for him. But will everyone recognize him? We have different expectations of God, and so different expectations of church. That's part of the problem. And to some extent, it's a problem between the generations. The God of the teenager is different from the God of children and the God of adults. Of course, there's only one God, but people see him and relate to him in different ways at different stages of their lives. And this affects their way of being religious and their expectations of church. If parent and child understand this, they have a much better chance to understand each other.

CHAPTER 5
A Case in Point

Young people of all denominations may stop attending church for any of the reasons mentioned to this point. But when a denomination undergoes extensive change, people of all ages may stop coming to church. Often they will contend that they have not really stopped attending church. It is just that the church they knew, loved, and attended is no longer there, it has changed so much. For such parents the matter of handing on the faith, of raising their children to attend church, is greatly complicated. The Roman Catholic Church from the mid-1960s to the present is a case in point.

Anyone who remembers what it was like to be a Catholic in 1960 knows that the Catholic Church has profoundly changed since that time. As much as possible, let's refrain from value judgements—whether these changes are beneficial or detrimental—and try simply to describe what has happened and what is going on, the better to assess its impact on the young.

The post-Vatican II changes have touched every phase of Catholic life, but the most obvious changes have occurred in the areas of liturgy and religious observance.

If Rip Van Winkle were Catholic and had slept from 1935 to 1955, he would, on awakening, have found that just about everything had changed except his church. But if he fell asleep in 1960 and awoke in 1980, it would be a far different story. In many ways, his church would be barely recognizable, at least on the surface. He would find that some of his old Catholic friends were disoriented and bitter about what had happened, while others were comfortable and even enthusiastic. But both groups, though disagreeing on almost everything else, would confide to Rip that it was getting harder and harder to bring up children in this "new" church. When pressed for an explanation, some would express the opinion that this was due not only to social and cultural upheavals in the larger society but in some way to the altered character of the church itself. Let's listen in on a conversation between Rip and a friend whom we shall describe as a progressive Catholic.

RIP VAN WINKLE: Do they still teach that missing Sunday Mass without an excuse is a serious sin?

PROGRESSIVE CATHOLIC FRIEND: Some do, but not nearly as many. A lot of us, including teachers and even priests, don't feel comfortable with that kind of motivation. We'd like people to come to church freely, not because they've been threatened.

RIP: As I remember it, those threats were pretty effective. The fear of hell got many a lazy person out of bed on Sunday morning.

P.C.F.: Well, Rip, you wouldn't have noticed it, but hell has been getting cooler every year.

RIP: That's no answer.

P.C.F.: No, of course not. But seriously, just how effective was that kind of negative motivation? Even in your time, fear could carry you over the short haul, but in the long run the only people who stayed with the church had something more going for them.

RIP: Like a sense of duty? Obligation?

P.C.F.: Yes, but an obligation of a certain kind; not an arbitrary imposition from the outside, but one that answers to human needs. Neglecting the Eucharist carries its own punishment: it's a form of spiritual starvation. If we refuse to hear the word of God or to eat the bread of life, we're hurting ourselves; we're punished already.

RIP: That's a good point. I never thought of it that way, but I guess you're right. Do you think kids can understand that?

P.C.F.: Ah, there's the problem. This is an adult conversation that you and I are having. The concept of obligation that I just expressed reflects a grown-up way of thinking that youngsters find hard to grasp.

RIP: Then perhaps we shouldn't talk this way to children, if it just confuses them. Maybe we should just tell them the law, explain the penalty, and put our foot down, the way we used to.

P.C.F.: It's not that easy, Rip. That'll work when the kids are too small to argue. At a very young age, they see all duty and obligation that way—as an arbitrary shape imposed on reality by the big people, especially parents. A four year old knows very well why it's wrong to run out on the road: because Mommy says so! At this age, breaking your sister's toys isn't wrong because your sister has rights and feelings; it's wrong because you'll get a spanking. Psychologists call this the premoral stage of development, when morality is just a matter of rewards and punishments. Good actions are the ones that earn you approval, and bad actions are the ones you get punished for. One obvious corollary is that it's okay if you don't get caught. Some adults never get beyond this stage of moral immaturity, and all of us lapse into it from time to time. But it's something to be outgrown.

RIP: So, instead of telling children something bad will happen to them if they miss Mass, you want to tell them why it's good to be there.

P.C.F.: Exactly.

RIP: Do you think they can understand?

P.C.F.: Yes, but in a limited way. The liturgy is not child's play, but something serious composed by adults for adults. Children, even older children and teenagers, usually don't understand why prayer and worship and the church's sacramental life are important. You need a certain amount of experience of life, a certain depth, to appreciate such things.

RIP: Indeed we do. I wonder how many adults reach this depth, this level of appreciation. Don't a great many folks go to church simply because they were taught that way and accept it without question?

P.C.F.: Yes, but have you noticed all those empty pews on Sunday? Young people are not the only ones who have dropped out, though they are the age group that is most conspicuous by its absence. In recent years a great many older Catholics who had nothing going for them but childhood indoctrination and ingrained religious habits have come up empty and drifted away.

RIP: What do you mean, come up empty?

P.C.F.: I mean they reached a point in their lives when they asked themselves, why am I doing this? As the Catholic ghetto began to break up, there was less and less social pressure to conform. There are people who like to think that they live the way they do not out of a desire to please others but from personal conviction, in accord with freely chosen values. We call them autonomous, inner-directed persons. When the only reasons they can think of for doing Catholic things are those that some authority figure told them a long time ago, when they realize that they are participating in church because it's expected of them or because it has become a habit, they feel hypocritical. So they drop out, or they drift off to the edges of the community, coming back only occasionally for guilt visits, when they feel more and more out of place.

RIP: That's an interesting theory. I don't

know how far it goes to explain adult religious alienation, but what does it have to do with the young?

P.C.F.: Plenty, if you think it through. Those adult fallen-away Catholics were once Catholic children and Catholic teenagers. Many, in their youth, were quite fervent and anxious to please. Something, though, went wrong, and it became painfully evident in their adult years. What do you think went wrong?

RIP: Oh, I suppose it could be many things: a neglect of prayer; the failure to cultivate a relationship with God; a lack of discipline; an uncritical acceptance of materialistic, anti-Christian values, with life-style to match. The list could go on and on. I still don't see what it tells us about our children.

P.C.F.: A few moments ago I said that children and adolescents are limited in their understanding and appreciation of an adult activity like the Eucharist. That's certainly true on the intellectual level. But on the level of feeling, some very solid—even profound—religious development can take place. Forget, for a moment, about the alienated and the dropouts, and consider those older adolescents and young adults who take religion seriously and are making progress toward a vigorous adult spirituality. When did these religious success stories start, if not in the impressionable years of childhood? And they began with more than a mastery of the catechism, more than just a cognitive grasp of religious information.

RIP: It must come down to the quality of experience, mustn't it? Some good things must have happened in the lives of those children, things they could build on as they grew older. If we could get a handle on just what those experiences are, and make them happen . . .

P.C.F.: We must be careful here to avoid some inviting traps. Faith, even in a child, is a very personal thing and cannot be totally programmed. It is also a free gift of God which must be freely accepted. Since it is also a relationship between persons, there can be no surefire formula for turning out Christians young or old.

RIP: Well said. Still, within such limits, we should be able to provide good religious experiences . . .

P.C.F.: Yes, sooner or later it must come to that. But we're getting ahead of ourselves. Before we talk about how to provide good religious experiences for the young, we must realize that these will not take place in a vacuum but within a community, a church. In trying to bring them up Catholic, we must prepare them to take their place not in the church that we knew but in the only church they will ever know—the church of the late twentieth and early twenty-first century. I wonder if you realize how deep the differences are.

RIP: Well, I'm certainly aware of them on Sunday. Hearing Mass in my own language, the priest facing the people, greeting people around me—that really threw me for a while. But I think I can adjust, and I may get to like it.

P.C.F.: I hope so. If you do, it will be because you see, under the changes, a continuity with something precious and enduring, something that was solemn and sacred and inspired reverence. The old liturgy, with its Latin, its elaborate and stylized ritual, the celebrant separate and remote, had its shortcomings. That's why it was changed. But it had some very real assets, too. It inspired a sense of the sacred and the mysterious. It spoke eloquently, in sign and symbol, of the holiness and transcendence of God. Even children sensed it; sometimes it was almost intimidating. What it lacked, of course, was participation and involvement; the celebrant did everything, while the people were passive spectators. And there was little sense of community among the worshipers. Where the changes have worked, communication has improved between celebrant and people: they have become more responsive to one another. That's what we call the *horizontal* dimension of the liturgy. But in the process we have sometimes lost the *vertical* dimension — that sense of the holy and the sacred, that feeling of reverential awe in the presence of God. It doesn't have to be that way, of course. Theoretically there's no reason why we can't pay attention to God and to one another at the same time. But it would be dishonest to deny that we often fail to put it all together.

RIP: I think I know what you mean. People do seem more relaxed in church, more at home. And there's something to be said for cultivating an easy familiarity with God. But sometimes I get the feeling that the only familiarity that's being cultivated is between people, and that God is almost forgotten. Maybe that's what the old-timers miss.

P.C.F.: Yes, the old-timers have their problems. They experience a sense of loss, a feeling that they had something good and beautiful and important, and that it's gone. The youngsters have problems, too, but they're quite different. A whole generation is coming to maturity that has no memory of the old Latin liturgy. They have no roots in the past, and they have been taught and trained by adults who were breaking with their past and going through their own identity crisis at a time when they should have come across as strong and self-assured role-models for the young. The results have often been disappointing; empty church pews are the most obvious but not the only evidence of this difficult transitional period in the life of the church.

RIP: Do kids still pray?

P.C.F.: That's a hard one to answer. Many of them do, in ways that are quite impressive. In many Catholic high schools, for example, there are elective courses where students can learn to pray. Some of them are quite popular.

RIP: They have to wait 'til high school? We learned when we were little.

P.C.F.: Rip, I don't know where to begin to explain. You and I memorized the Our Father and the Hail Mary, the Creed, and other prayers. We defined prayer as "raising the mind and heart to God." There were set times for prayer—at rising and before retiring, before class, before and after meals. That sort of thing still goes on, but it may be dying out.

RIP: Why?

P.C.F.: Well, that kind of prayer was tied to a whole way of thinking about God and relating to him—a religious culture, if you will. Serious religious people became aware of some of its more glaring limitations. A God to whom we "raised" our minds and hearts was psychologically "up there," far away, uninvolved in life. But God isn't distant, he's in all reality: he *is* reality. As St. Augustine says, he is closer to us than our most intimate selves. In a very special way he is present in other persons, so that we meet him in one another. Being attentive and sensitive to one another becomes, in a very real sense, a prayer. There's that horizontal dimension again.

RIP: That sounds a lot like what we used to call humanism. I've known many atheists and agnostics who say they aren't interested in God, they're interested in people. They care about others and do a lot of good for them, but they aren't religious.

P.C.F.: Funny you should mention the humanists. When you watch some of our young doing what they call religion, you have to wonder how it's any different. Observe, for example, how they "rate" a liturgy. A good celebration, for them, is one in which people come to feel more united, less constrained, closer to one another. That is certainly a most desirable outcome of liturgy, but is it the only one? Couldn't you accomplish the same thing in an encounter group, a concert, or a social? Sometimes when they complain about "getting nothing out of" Mass, they are using a very narrow standard. Or listen to a group of teenagers who have just returned, all enthusiastic, from one of their popular weekend retreats. Some obviously good things have happened to them in the area of human relationships; but are those experiences properly called religious? It's not always clear; but the question deserves to be asked.

RIP: Do they say the same prayers we learned as kids?

P.C.F.: By the time they're teenagers, they resist the idea of reciting memorized prayers. Set prayers seem artificial and rote, lacking in spontaneity. So does a schedule, a determined time and place for praying. This is probably an overreaction to formalistic, mechanical patterns of religiosity. It's all right provided youngsters learn how to pray in their own words and in their own way. It's a skill that has to be learned; people don't come by it naturally. That's why they have those high school prayer courses.

RIP: Let me see if I can put some of this together. You have been describing a new way of bringing up young church members. You want them to come to church out of love, not out of fear. You want them to see obligation as something built into reality, not imposed on it. Instead of indoctrinating them early and giving them good religious habits, you hope that they will become Christian by personal conviction and free choice. You imply that very early experiences of prayer and worship, especially within the family, are crucial to this development. You say they are sensitive to the demands of human relationships, but find it hard to relate to the transcendent, so that their religious style is much more horizontal than vertical. Finally, they put a high value on spontaneity and feel phony when saying memorized prayers or sticking to a set time or place for religious activity. Is that an accurate picture of the youth scene in today's church?

P.C.F.: Allowing for the inevitable exceptions, yes.

RIP: Do you honestly think we can make all that happen? Since kids are, by definition, immature, I wonder if they can handle it. Aren't we going to lose a lot of them?

P.C.F.: I don't know if we can make it happen. The new approach is ambitious. Kids are immature. A good many of them can't handle it, and that's why we're losing them.

RIP: And yet you persist.

P.C.F.: What choices do we have? To go back to 1950? It wouldn't work; it's a different world—maybe not better, but different. We can't go back. We have to meet kids where they are, introduce them to God, and help them find him in ways different from the ways we learned. We must challenge them, correct them, encourage them, being ever true to our own convictions. Sure, they have to learn; but so do we. The day we stop growing and learning, we're dead. Some of the kids think we're already a bunch of stiffs.

RIP: It seems to me that you're asking a lot not only of the kids but of the grown-ups, too.

P.C.F.: Yes, and not just of the teachers. No matter how well the youngsters are taught their religion, the payoff depends on the quality of adult faith that they see around them. Today's exodus of young people from the church is due, at least in part, to deficiencies in the adult Catholic community. Unless young people see, in that community, signs of life, like conviction, joy, openness, care, and a hunger for justice, they will continue to leave. Some of those signs of life should be evident on Sunday morning, but they need to spill over into the rest of the week, too.

RIP: So changes in the liturgy are only the tip of the iceberg. There has been a revolution in the way people think about God and relate to him, and in the way they pray and worship. But that isn't the whole story, is it?

P.C.F.: No, the effects have been felt in other areas of Catholic life, too. Especially in morality: the way we think and feel about right and wrong and sin and penance and judgement. But that's another whole story.

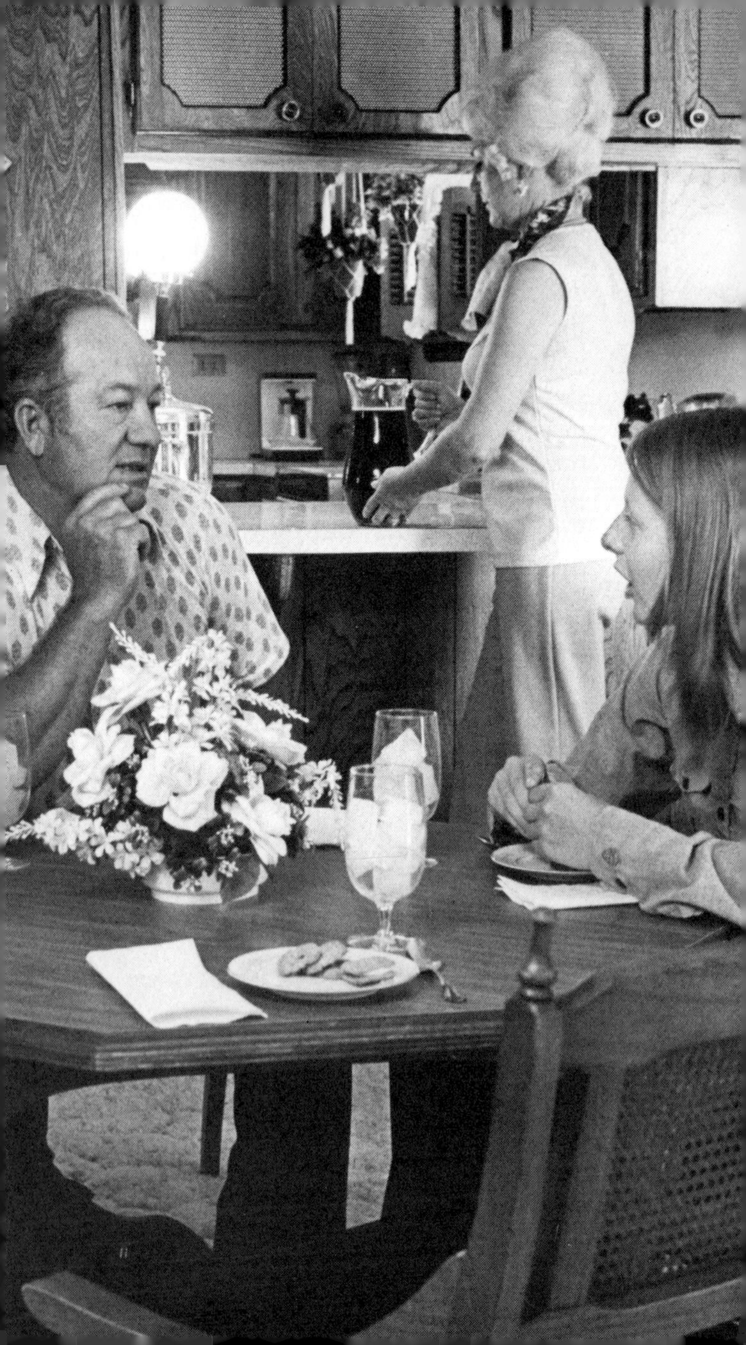

CHAPTER 6
Authority and Freedom

The attitude of young people toward religion is deeply influenced by their understanding of right and wrong, their concept of morality. There are two basic ways of approaching a question of morality. One is rooted in authority, the other in freedom. One is known as *legalistic* or *juridical:* There is the law, and anyone who knows the law, seriously reflects upon it in a given situation, and gives full consent to a contrary action is guilty of breaking the law, of committing an immoral act. The other approach is called *personalistic:* It starts not from laws, but from persons. It concentrates not on individual acts, but on patterns of living. It sees sin not as the breaking of a law but as the weakening or destruction of a relationship.

The differences between these two approaches is illustrated by an experience I had a few years ago. A mother of one of my high school students was sure her son had done something seriously sinful in not attending church on Sunday. He was honestly baffled by his mother's attitude, and I had to explain to him what was behind his mother's thinking. I think he finally understood her position, but he could not identify with it.

For the mother, it was very simple. Not attending church on Sunday without a good reason is seriously sinful when it is truly willful, and this was evidently the case since the boy could come up with no acceptable excuse.

The mother in her legalistic approach to morality could not escape her judgment about the moral significance of her son's absence from church. Legalists discover serious sin much more easily than personalists, who start from different premises, ask different questions, and (not surprisingly) come up with different answers. A personalist would want to know much more about the boy—whether he usually went to church, how important it was to him, what one Sunday's absence meant in the total context of his lived relationship with Christ and his Church. Because personalists concentrate not on individual acts in isolation but on the broader context in which those acts take place, their conclusions are usually less definite.

Young people growing up today are meeting fewer legalists and more personalists. Many learn about sin and guilt and repentance in ways and in language quite different from that of their parents. Are they better off? Is the new way an improvement? In some ways, yes; but the picture is mixed. Personalism demands a certain maturity, a degree of sophistication not required by legalism. Rules and penalties are more easily understood by children than are the demands of relationships; that's why it's much easier to teach them the old way.

This illustrates a phenomenon that has been alluded to more than once in this book: the difficulty of translating adult religion into language that children and adolescents will not misunderstand. Tell a group of high school students that not attending church once on a Sunday is not necessarily seriously sinful, and some will conclude that it's okay to stay home, period. Tell them that sin consists not in breaking rules but in using and hurting people, and they'll decide that premarital sex is okay as long as you really "love" the other person and nobody gets hurt. There's a certain amount of self-deception and dishonesty at work here, as well as immaturity. Self-serving people hear pretty much what they want to hear. Once you admit that sin is not as easy to determine as we once thought, it's a small step to saying, in effect, that there isn't any sin at all.

This problem is intensified by the fact that in our culture people are uncomfortable with the word "sin." The experience of guilt is suspect. Guilt, in the popular mind, has been uncritically dismissed as neurotic. We wouldn't dream of imposing on our children some of the guilt trips that we took in our youth. This is especially true in the matter of sex. It goes without saying that the results of this are neither all good nor all bad. We are well rid of some of our old hang-ups, but we are not clearly better off: witness the shambles of contemporary sexual standards.

The effect of all this on the young is not easily detected; you have to know where to look. Notice the words that they do *not* use: sin, evil, responsible, right, wrong. In the vocabulary of youth, people do not commit sin or do evil; they are "sick." Muggers are sick; rapists are sick — a very interesting and revealing word! Do we blame people for being ill? Are sick people free? And if they're not, how can they be responsible? How can anyone be condemned for anything? Why should they be sorry, and how can they repent when it wasn't their fault? There's nothing to confess, and nothing to forgive, when you follow this line of reasoning. Ask the kids about right and wrong, and they'll ask you — right for whom? Who can say what's right or wrong for another person? Isn't it all relative?

These points of view were repeatedly voiced in conversations I have had with teenagers over several years. The ideas expressed are simplistic, shallow, and naive. They tell us something about the difficulties involved in growing up and becoming a morally mature human being. The confusion of youth mirrors the confusion in adult society, where consensus has broken down and many are adrift. The confusion reaches them through the media of mass culture—television, movies, music, magazines. To people who accept these values and attitudes, the very language that religion uses in discussing morality is at best quaint and at worst incomprehensible.

In the past, religious conferences with youth have mostly focused on sex and sin and guilt and forgiveness. (Even when the leader didn't talk sex, that's what the kids heard.) Remember the question box and the question most often submitted: How far can you go on a date without committing serious sin? That world has disappeared. But what has taken its place? As long as we asked the old questions we could get young people deeply involved in church. As long as sex was dangerous, sin was real, hell was hot, and God wasn't fooling around, religion was played for high stakes. Now sex is no big deal, sin is hardly mentioned, hell is cooling off, and God gets more tolerant every year. One thing is sure: ministering to the religious needs of young people today calls for new skills and even a new language. Such skills are in short supply among those who work with the young, and will be for some time.

Many parents whose children stop going to church feel not only disappointed and guilty but also angry at those who were supposed to help—

religious educators. Why didn't they do for my kid what my teachers did for me? Teachers today cannot simply repeat for their students the things they were told when they were in school. The message is fundamentally the same, but the milieu is so different that the tasks of catechesis and moral education are profoundly altered.

If you talk to as many teachers as I do, you get the same story in reverse. They are disappointed in parents. How, they ask, can they make up in one or a few hours a week for all that their students' parents have failed to do the rest of the time? Sometimes parents underrate the challenge of religious formation, and leave to the classroom more than the teacher can deliver. Some teachers are poorly equipped, either through lack of training or because they don't know how to adapt to the real needs of growing children.

There are many well-educated and idealistic religion teachers who want their students to become persons of integrity with their own clearly defined set of values, and able to live in a manner consistent with these values. They see the truly moral person not as a blind follower or as one ruled by fear, but as a genuinely free man or woman making moral decisions as a responsible individual. These teachers try not so much to impose the truth as to create learning situations in which students can discover the truth for themselves. They seek not to program people for conformity but to liberate them so that they can be persons of conscience who act on principle. Teachers don't help produce such people by making pronouncements, laying down the law, discouraging discussion, and penalizing dissent. Rather they must create a classroom climate of acceptance that encourages questioning and respects individual differences. This calls for great skill and the taking of calculated risks.

Some teachers fail to perceive these risks. They are so wary of imposing their own beliefs, so reluctant to short-circuit discussion, that they fail to challenge students who come up with half-baked, potentially destructive ideas. Half the class comes away with the impression that anything goes, that there's no one right answer to any question, that everyone is free to do his or her own thing. And when they voice such impressions at home, the parents wonder what the teachers are presenting at school.

Teachers who make these mistakes are not wrong in the goals they pursue. They are right in their conviction that religious education programs must educate not for conformity but for free choice. But those educators who perceive their profession as a liberating one must take into account the limitations of their pupils. In this matter, help has come from the work of developmental psychologists like Dr. Lawrence Kohlberg, who has elaborated a stage theory of moral development widely accepted in scientific and academic circles. According to Kohlberg, children's earliest moral judgments and decisions are made in terms of reward and punishment. Later, right and wrong become functions of the expectations of significant others—parents, peers, society. At the highest level of moral maturity—a level most adults fail to reach, according to Kohlberg—the person judges and acts in accord with universal principles of justice. It is this last stage of maturity that educators take as the goal for their students. But in encouraging and promoting this development, they must be mindful of some of Kohlberg's cautions. According to his stage theory, people are limited in their ability to grasp levels of motivation higher than their present stage of development. Thus, if a student is at the reward-punishment stage, it is futile and misleading to appeal to conscience in the sense of personal moral conviction. Tell some youngsters they should "follow their conscience" and what they hear is "you can do as you please."

Adapting to the students' limited development is not as easy as it sounds. Suppose you want to motivate teenagers to refrain from premarital sex. If they are at the lower levels of maturity (and most of them are), they can understand warnings against pregnancy and venereal disease, but will have difficulty grasping the deeper considerations underlying traditional sexual standards. The demands of loving relationships—honesty, commitment, fidelity, unselfishness—are not easily understood or appreciated by immature teenagers. Even their budding sensitivity to such motives often caves in under the tremendous pressure from peers and the mass media to engage in premarital intimacy. As a result, the reasons that a teacher finds most cogent and convincing are the ones least likely to be understood.

A major obstacle to the sound moral guidance of youth comes from our materialistic culture. The not-so-hidden message of the mass media and advertising, especially that aimed at youth, is that real living means getting the most you can, any way you can, and right away if not sooner. You are what you own. If you're not getting sex or trying to get it, there's something wrong with you. Postponing gratification is bad for you. It's a rare kid, or grown-up for that matter, who is totally untouched by this plastic gospel. Now consider the moral message of religion. What does it say? A great big "No" to everything the hucksters and the disc jockeys and your peers say you just gotta have. Being Christian could cost you. Is it any wonder so many want to split?

The question of authority in the Church has to be considered in coming to grips with the question of youth who stop going to church. Few young people feel that any church leader has anything to say that will touch their lives. And, in a way, they're right. But as we pointed out earlier, they won't be kids forever; and if they are going to maintain any connection with the Church, they will have to come to terms with authority. How shall we present that authority to them?

If we present the old authoritarian image of church leaders as people appointed to settle disputes and whose word is final, we shall at least be understood. Youngsters can grasp that kind of job description. To them, all authorities—parents, principals, presidents—are the ones who have the power and can make decisions stick. There's no point in arguing. You can't fight city hall. Love it or leave it. The only alternatives are running away from home, dropping out of school, or leaving church.

There's another way of presenting church authority, not as easily understood but more in keeping with a responsible adult view of church. In this approach the job of church officials from the top down is not to terminate disputes and impose settlements, but to preach the gospel in season and out of season. This means challenging people with Christ's values and encouraging them to seek the guidance of the Holy Spirit. It includes taking stands and saying things that some people don't want to hear. But it respects individual consciences, can live with dissent, and calls upon adult Christians to take responsibility for their decisions and their lives. This kind of authority does not try to relieve people of the burden of thinking and deciding and living with the consequences of their choices. It does not try to destroy conscience or to substitute for it. It plays the prophet, not the tyrant. It demands no oath of loyalty except to Christ.

This second shape and style of authority is the only one that makes any sense to growing numbers of adult Christians, but it is difficult to present to young people. Most of them seem puzzled and confused by it. It isn't a matter of intelligence: many of these youngsters are bright, well-motivated students. Yet they cannot comprehend the notion of a church authority that is open, broad-minded, and liberal rather than rigid and repressive. There are two reasons for the difficulty young people have with this approach.

The first has to do with their own immaturity. Developmental psychologists point to a stage in people's lives where their religious or moral convictions are based on some uncritically accepted authority. This authority may take the form of a pope or a national government or the head of some valued institution. The key word is *uncritical*. When this authority speaks clearly, dissent is unthinkable. When the boss speaks, that settles it, period. Many citizens look upon the government this way. If drafted to serve in war, they cannot conceive of doing anything but obeying: "My country, right or wrong." Kohlberg calls this the law-and-order stage of moral maturity, and his research has convinced him that only a minority of adults ever go beyond it. I have encountered this mentality many times in discussing with adult Catholics the roles of conscience and authority in the church particularly in the question of birth control. No matter how carefully I expressed the individual's obligation to consider carefully the pope's teaching before making a decision, they heard me saying, "Then you can do as you please." Well, if adults are limited in this way, what can we expect of adolescents? As the latter see it, you either belong to the church and submit to authority, or you leave it and are free. The idea of being a loyal and committed Catholic and yet free and responsible is too paradoxical for their young minds to comprehend.

The second reason young people have trouble with an approach to church authority that underscores their freedom cannot be described in a word, but in a behavior pattern that we have all observed in very small children and which has been duly noted and analyzed by child psychologists. Toddlers love to roam and to meander off to strange and exciting places beyond their parents' watchful eyes and secure grasp. But have you ever seen one of these little wanderers return and not find Mommy or Daddy right where they left him or her? Howls of resentment! The parents have violated a sacred rule: Kids may wander off but parents must stay put. I have the very definite impression, reinforced by innumerable encounters with teenagers, that the Church for them is a parent that is not supposed to move. An unbending, inflexible church is one they can handle. Such an institution is easy to reject. But a church that evolves, that grows, that is open to change and learns from criticism and experience—a church that *moves*—they don't know what to do with that.

CHAPTER 7
What to Do

Getting young people to church is not a nuts-and-bolts problem like fixing a car or buying a house. There are no "three easy steps" to follow. It's not just a "how-to" but also a "what-for" question of intangibles like identity, and values, and meaning.

The first thing to remember is that not all young people are the same, and that their reasons for leaving church are many and varied. In Chapter Two we discussed several of these. They suggest the key questions to ask before you decide on a strategy. Is your son or daughter rejecting church or religion or both? Is the action an isolated phenomenon, or part of a pattern of rejection of family values and life-styles? Does the impulse come from within the person, or is it the result of peer pressure? Is he or she a leader or a follower? What is your relationship with this member of your family? Some children need and subconsciously want a firm hand; they want you to take the lead, even while they fight for every inch of ground. Other children, often within the same family, have to be handled quite differently; the more you insist the farther you drive them away. There is no one formula for every parent and child, even within the same home.

Sometimes the best thing to do with a child who resists churchgoing is simply to insist, "You're going, and that's that." This is often the case with preteens and early teens. At this age their resistance may be capricious and childish, with no depth. Although some people, whose opinion cannot be easily dismissed, feel that any kind of religious coercion is unwise, I cannot agree. There are many things that children of this age should do but don't want to, and many things they want to do but shouldn't. Some of them would live on hamburgers and fries and Coke if they had their way; wise parents insist on a balanced diet. They'd stay out till all hours if their parents lacked the courage to say no. How many would go to school and study and do homework without the firm guidance of parents and other caring adults?

So the first time your twelve year old asks, "Why do we have to go to church?" your answer is, "Because it's important." You may or may not enlarge on that answer, as you wish. Just don't say, "Because you must" or "Because it's sinful not to." That creates many problems and solves none. It gives the impression that the operative motive, for you as well as for them, is *fear*. Such negative motivation wipes out, in the youngster's mind, all other considerations, including the positive ones for going. If you have to go to church to stay out of hell, why bother looking for reasons why it's good to go?

Rather than threatening them, it's much more effective to make the point that worship is important to you personally. Since they were very small, your children have been picking up signals from you about what's good and bad and important and unimportant. Visiting Grandma is important. Eating your vegetables is important. So is telling the truth, and cleaning your room, and going to school. All their young lives you have been teaching them values. By now they know that there are certain things you would never do and that you would feel bad if they did them, such as missing church. They are too young to fully understand your reasons, and they don't have to. It doesn't matter whether the reasons you give would pass inspection in a graduate theology course. For when your son or daughter asks, "why do we have to . . . ?," they're not initiating a theological discussion. What they really want to know is where you stand and how much you're going to let them get away with.

So, from the beginning, make it clear that if they skip church and you find out, they're in

WHAT TO DO

trouble—but with you, not with God. Sure, God wants them there, too, but it would not be helpful to dwell on that. He wants them there for *their* sake, but that's hard for them to understand, just as it's hard for them to understand that you make them do many things for their own good. It's enough for them now to know that you take God seriously, that liturgy is an important part of your relationship with him, and that you want them to share it.

When they get older you may have to go deeper and explain more. But by that time hopefully their experiences will have provided them with reasons of their own. If it hasn't—if religion and church have not been experienced as somehow enriching their lives—then they probably won't accept anyone else's reasons.

Sometimes the problem does not go so deep. It may not be church or faith as such that is causing the problem for your son or daughter, but just the local situation. Perhaps the liturgy is badly celebrated, the services are boring, or perhaps there is nothing provided for young people. Some parishes are lifeless communities that limp along without enthusiasm or inspiration. The solution may be to go to a neighboring church where there is a better spirit or where young people feel more welcome. Such "shopping around" should not be done lightly. But institutions exist for people, not vice-versa. If a young person or a whole family has to find another parish to receive necessary spiritual help, then they should do it with regret but without guilt.

Maybe your instincts as a parent tell you that the tactics suggested thus far simply are not right for you. You may suspect that insisting on church attendance is going to prove counterproductive, and you may be right. You know your child and your relationship better than anyone else. Perhaps it is best to be silent or to look the other way, lest you win the battle and lose the war. There are times in the life of every adolescent when he or she needs some room. The task of establishing an adult identity involves rebelling against a dependent position. We are not surprised when adolescents resist our wishes and try to assert their independence. But when they do so in religious matters, there is usually additional emotional impact that makes it more threatening. In our wiser moments we know it is well that they seek their independence, no matter how much pain or worry may be in it for us. We are most prudent if we know when to beat a strategic retreat and leave the field to fight another day, to simply leave them alone.

But can you prevent this retreat from being a full-scale capitulation? There are ways, as long as a serious conversation is still possible between you and your teenager. Once it is clear that you're not going to make an issue of regular churchgoing, at least for now, you are in the diplomatic position of having made a concession. Instead of playing the heavy, you have been the good guy. This gives you a chance to ask some serious questions without recrimination.

    1) *Now that you have dropped church from your life, what are you putting in its place?*

If the answer is "nothing" or a blank stare, then,

    2) *What are you doing for the spiritual side of yourself?*

This may seem an unlikely script for the average American family, but consider for a moment. No one thinks it inappropriate for a parent to make inquiries about career plans, or the choice of a high school or college, or the state of a growing child's physical health. If it's not taboo to talk about these things, why can't we talk about spiritual health or religious development? If the answer to this unconventional inquiry is the conventional adolescent rejoinder that "you don't have to go to church to be religious or a good person," you can agree and then return to question #2 which has still not been answered, namely, "What are you doing? Do you, for instance, pray?"

The answer may come back, "You don't have to go to church to pray. You can pray in your room."

"True, Well, do you?"

"Do what?"

"Pray in your room." (Silence.) "When? How?" (Deep silence.) "Do you intend to cultivate your spiritual self as a purely private project, or are you planning to join a cult? Have you looked into TM or est or any other group?"

That last part may sound sarcastic, but it doesn't have to be. Any kid who has anything besides the top 40 tunes on his or her mind knows that many people in our society become grasping, shallow, one-dimensional materialists. I've never yet met a young person who said that this is a good thing. So you and your child have something in common: you agree that there's more to living than grabbing and getting and consuming. You look to your church to help you broaden your world, your aspirations and concerns. What does your son or daughter look to?

If you can have a conversation like this, you will no longer be on the defensive. Instead of fighting the losing battle of trying to defend or excuse all the real and imagined shortcomings of the Church, you have sent the ball into your son's or daughter's court. He or she has to come up with answers to some down-to-earth questions. Don't let your child avoid facing the questions. Suppose your teenager became a vegetarian and refused to eat meat because he or she was against killing living things. It's a no-win proposition to try to come up with arguments in favor of killing animals. Rather, confront your son or daughter with the question of how he or she is going to get enough protein to make up for the loss from not eating meat.

When you talk this way to young adults, you are no longer saying, in effect, "You have to be like me!" but rather "What do you want to be?" Rebellion is childish when it knows only what it is against, and doesn't know what it seeks.

Sometimes there are more people involved than you and your teenage son or daughter. If there are younger children in the family, how do we explain to them their older brother's or sister's absence from church? If we say they can stay away because they're older, we risk giving the impression that one of the advantages of growing up is that you can drop church. For this reason, some parents tell or ask their older children to go to church for the sake of the younger ones. Often they will go along with this, from a protective instinct or out of consideration for their parents' feelings. This is alright as long as we recognize it for what it is — a stopgap measure and not a solution. The high school junior or senior who accepts this compromise may be away at college or have his or her own apartment in a year or two, and then there will be nothing to get them to church except their own convictions and sense of responsibility. Before that time, we should try to have some serious and constructive discussion along the lines described above. Otherwise we are avoiding or postponing problems instead of facing them.

In planning your strategy, you must make a decision about just where the problem lies. Is your son or daughter rejecting only church, or the very idea of religion? This is not an idle question. I have known many young people who take quite seriously the religious dimension of their lives and who are open to ways of expressing it, but who cannot see the Church helping them in this regard. In such cases it is necessary to talk about church, to help them develop reasonable expectations of church leaders and communities, and to find a vital local church community that will respond to their needs.

On the other hand, many youngsters' neglect or rejection of church is rooted in an inability to take seriously any kind of religion or religious activity. This is more serious, for it involves a whole way of relating to life. In such cases parents should ask certain fundamental questions. I have found that these questions are not:

>Is there a God?
>What is he like?
>Does Jesus reveal him?
>How do we follow Jesus?

but rather:

>What do you want out of life?
>What will you need to be happy?
>What kind of person are you becoming?
>What kind of person do you want to be?

Until these questions can be asked and responded to, religious questions are idle word games, religious obligations are meaningless, and the kindest thing you can say about religious activity is that it is a distraction. Asking these questions in serious dialogue can initiate a

WHAT TO DO

process whereby your son or daughter can establish religion as a vital part of life. Don't hesitate to share your own personal religious quest in dealing with such questions.

One final practical suggestion, which may work when all of the above have failed. Why not ask your son or daughter to read this book and discuss it with you. Such dialogue is not easy to carry on with a young person. For that matter, not many Americans, young or old, are comfortable discussing religion on a personal level. But if both of you (or the three of you, including your spouse) could treat this book as a conversation starter, some good things could happen. It at least gives you a shared language and point of reference. Some skill is required to get such a discussion off the ground. Here is one way *not* to begin:

YOU: What did you think of the book?
OFFSPRING: It was okay, I guess.
YOU: Did it help at all?
OFFSPRING: Nah. Listen, I gotta go. I'll see you.

End of discussion.

When you discuss the book, be more specific. "Was there anything in the book that you agreed with? What, exactly?" "Anything that you disagreed with? What?" "Did you see yourself, or us, described anywhere?" If you're still getting only vague generalities, pick out some passages that particularly spoke to you and ask for a reaction. Choose a time when neither of you is in a hurry, and a setting where you can both be relaxed and serious. Do at least as much listening as talking. Don't settle for a passive, defensive position on your son's or daughter's part. Seek a person-to-person conversation about serious, adult matters; kid-style behavior is out of place.

Of course, this puts some pressure on you, too. You cannot insist that the discussion go your way and turn out as you plan. You have to be open and respectful of the other's right to reach conclusions different from your own. That entails a risk, to be sure, but at least you will have begun to talk with, not at, each other; and that is no small thing. It might even be the first step toward a happy ending—not right away, but in God's good time.

CHAPTER 8
Letting Go

In the previous chapters of this book we have examined the religious alienation of young people—why it happens, what it means, and what we can do about it. Hopefully, these chapters have enabled you to put into perspective your son's or daughter's rejection of church. You may have picked up some constructive suggestions for dealing with your teenage children or with other members of your family, especially the younger children. Perhaps you have taken a new look at the way you are living out your own religious commitment. If you see yourself as part of the problem, some changes may be called for in your own relationship with God and the Church. None of these outcomes can, by itself, heal the wound of separation, but they may hold out hope for a better future and even for reconciliation.

"But what if my child's estrangement from church is final and irrevocable, and I cannot do anything about it?" It should be noted that sometimes the break will prove not to be as final as we may have thought. Many young people neglect church in high school or drop out altogether in college years. But with marriage or the birth of children young couples find themselves returning to the institutional church to celebrate, in symbol and ceremony, the most solemn and significant events in their lives. Regardless of their expressed motivation at the time, "We're being married in church because my parents want us to" or, "We're having the baby christened because the grandparents expect it," the occasion can be one of religious renewal. When this happens we should not criticize or blame them for having neglected their religious obligations, but rather speak of how easy it is to lose contact with the Church in the crowded years of young adulthood, amid the distractions of education, career beginnings, dating, and courtship. The occasion of their renewed interest should never be an occasion for reproach, but rather should be treated as an opportunity for them to take a fresh look at the Christian faith in which you raised them. The rebelliousness of adolescence is past and they are putting down roots and investing in the future. From this vantage point, religion may look quite different from what it did a few years previously. The time may be ripe for them and the

Church to give each other a second chance.

Holding out this kind of hope may seem like wishful thinking. But it is supported by something we know, from psychology and observation, about adolescents and young adults. They have a need to break away from persons and things in their lives, to reject dependence and establish autonomy, in order to be able to return later on their own terms. So many of the things that touch their very identity—their values, their aspirations, their moral standards, their religion—have been *given* to them by parents and teachers and other adults. It is natural and healthy for these young people on the threshold of adulthood to want to assert their independence. Sometimes they do this in ways that cause us pain—leaving home, refusing assistance, dropping out of church. Most of these ruptures need not be final. Once they have proved that they can "make it on their own," they can come home again without losing face. It is the wise parent who can see these apparent rejections for what they are and who knows when to let go. As a teacher, I have concluded after years of experience that many of my teenage students are bound to reject a certain amount of what I teach them precisely because it comes from someone they consider an authority figure.

Suppose there is no realistic expectation of your children being reconciled to the church: everything tells you that the break is final. It is important for you to remember that faith is not so much a *given* as it is a *project*. You cannot "give" a child faith and then demand that he or she not "lose" it. Faith is something to be achieved through openness to God's grace, and the process is never completed until life is over. It is rooted in experience, and depends on encounter and sharing in order to blossom out into a mature and enduring relationship. It is personal and unique and totally free; hence it cannot be infallibly programmed or accurately judged by any human being. So when religion doesn't "take" with a young person, go easy on the guilt, and don't torture yourself with remorse that is not deserved. We have absolutely no right to accuse or judge those who drop out of the Church altogether, for we cannot possibly know how they stand in God's eyes. Regret and sorrow, yes; guilt and condemnation, no.

Some who read this may feel comforted but confused. They may hear us saying that being a Christian is important, but that missing out on the chance is nothing to worry about. Isn't that a contradiction? No, but it is a paradox. There's a subtle but crucial difference, which we'll try to explain.

All Christians believe that the ultimate destiny of human beings is to come to eternal life in the kingdom of God. We are made in God's image and likeness, and are meant to share his life in the most intimate and fulfilling way. The achievement of this goal is popularly called "heaven," which we tend to imagine as a place, but which we know is a state of existence beyond all our imagining and comprehension. Since we are created free, this magnificent destiny is not forced upon us; we must choose life. God does not conscript us, he invites us; and he will settle for nothing less than a totally free response. Salvation is not an achievement but a gift graciously offered to us by a loving Father who regards not our sinfulness but only our openness to his love.

At the center of Christian tradition is the conviction that salvation comes through Jesus Christ. By his death and resurrection he overcomes the power of sin and death and offers the fullness of life. This life is mediated through a believing and worshiping community called the Church, whose members are the very body of Christ, making him and his power present and active in the world. We Christians consider ourselves blessed in a special way because we have received the gift of faith within the community of those who acknowledge the lordship of Jesus. This does not mean that we are better than others or that God loves us more. We simply acknowledge with gratitude the fact that, through no merit of ours, we have come to know Christ and consciously to share his life within the Church. It is this gift that we try to share with our children when we baptize them and bring them up as Christians.

Now the key question is: How does membership in the community of Christ's disciples affect our chances for salvation? Or, to put it in other words, what is the relationship between church and kingdom? Must we belong to the Church in order to attain eternal life? These are questions, debated among theologians, which become very practical for us when those we love abandon the Church.

One opinion, held from time to time by a few but always rejected by the Church at large, answers that salvation is attainable only through *explicit* membership in the Church. Another opinion, more widely held and always respected, holds that *implicit* membership in the Church is necessary for salvation. This is interpreted not as an exclusion of non-Christians from the kingdom but as an indication that men and women of goodwill who respond to God's grace in their lives, belong to the Church without realizing it. They are called "anonymous Christians." Some of this second group think that many of those who leave the Church have never been effectively evangelized and do not know Christ well enough to reject him. (In my years of teaching in Catholic high schools, I believe I have encountered thousands of youngsters who fit this description.) Such persons, in this view, can also be considered implicit members of the Church because their apparent rejection of it arises from blameless ignorance.

A third view is at once more radical and simple. It holds that while all men and women are called by God to the kingdom, not all are called to the Church. The expression "outside the Church no salvation" means not that all must somehow belong to the Church in order to be saved, but that the world will not be saved without the Church. Belonging to this Church does not give us a head start toward salvation, but rather imposes on us the duty to go out to the world and serve all God's children, both those who know him and those who do not. I call this a *centrifugal* rather than a *centripetal* vision of church, which sees the followers of Christ not as a group huddling together to escape damnation, but as a select army with a mission to serve. Richard McBrien, one of the leading exponents of this approach, sees the Christian community as summoned to be a light to the gentiles, a "model city" holding out hope and inspiration to a tired, cynical, despairing world.

Whichever one of these last two views seems preferable, it is important to note that both have great respect for the infinite variety of paths that lead to God. We must take care not to esteem these less than God does. To speak thus is not to make light of the gift of faith but to make room for God's magnanimity. Many, including perhaps our children, are on their way to the kingdom of God along paths that look very different from our own. We all know people, young and old, who do not share our faith but whose lives are exemplary and even inspiring. They are loving, caring generous souls who leave the world a little better than they found it. They often put us to shame as they live up to Christian values better than we do, even as they call them by other names. Whether they are anonymous Christians or people called to the kingdom and not to the Church, they are making progress toward becoming the kind of person Jesus wanted us to be, and they are doing it in response to his grace. It is hard to believe that Christ loves them any less because they do not know his name or where to find him.

The last thing that needs to be said, before we close, is that God wants us to believe not only in him but also in ourselves and in one another. This book was written for, and will be read by, people who are experiencing the pain of separation. We have tried not to make light of that separation or to deny the pain. We have offered no cheap consolation, no dishonest assurances, or vague pieties. How we and our children respond to Christ's summons to decision is the most important thing we will do in our lives. Religion is played for high stakes; there are losers as well as winners. Let's hope that these pages, with God's help, will make a few more winners. Meanwhile, as we pray for one another without ceasing, let us be humble and patient and wait for God, in his good time, to end all separation and bring us and our families back together in his loving embrace.